THE LITTLE BOOK

OF HAPPINESS

Affirmations That Can Help You

Have A Brighter Day!

By

Martin H. Pye

Disclaimer: This book is not intended as a substitute for the advice of mental health professionals.

TABLE OF CONTENTS

OTHER TITLES BY THE AUTHOR

TAKE ACTION AND CHANGE: Be the Best Version of Yourself

"You have power over your mind – not outside events. Realize this, and you will find strength."

- Marcus Aurelius -

INTRODUCTION

Welcome to The Little Book of Happiness. This will not be a long-winded read, but rather a straight-to-the-point reference book that you can carry around on your person and refer to as and when you need it. Inside you will find plenty of affirmations for you to use that will inspire you to seize the day.

I love helping people to realise that they are unique and can achieve amazing results when they recognize their own worth. Therefore, it is my mission to help others overcome any feelings of inadequacy and to aid them in understanding that we all deserve to feel love within ourselves.

The book is broken down into specific areas of life that the majority of people focus upon. This makes it easier for you to navigate and find what you are looking for. There are sections that require you to write down what you are aiming for in life, and to create your own personalized affirmations.

Enjoy reading this little book and carry it around with you. Use it as a daily guide and take control of your life.

FOCUS ON WHAT YOU CAN CONTROL

Before moving on to the affirmations, let us discuss the importance of placing your focus on the four areas listed in this section.

It is so easy to become overwhelmed with everything going on in life whether it affects you directly or not. Therefore, you must come to terms with the idea that it is far healthier for your wellbeing to focus on the things that you have control over. These areas include:

Your Mindset

Keep everything as positive as you possibly can. When you begin to possess a happy and enthusiastic attitude you will start noticing that you feel better about yourself, you smile more often, and you don't get easily overwhelmed.

Others notice and enjoy being around positive and happy people. So, drop the doom and gloom and turn your attention towards being a friendly and approachable person with a good attitude.

Stop giving attention to what other people think about you. Obviously, this is aimed at the opinions of those who may not like you, feel jealousy toward you, or are simply just toxic individuals. When you stop paying attention to what others think about you, it allows you to start seeing life from a new and exciting perspective. You begin living for yourself and have a lot more fun instead of worrying about what others are saying or thinking. You do things because you want to do them on your terms, rather than do them to appease those who judge you.

General Wellness

Start training a healthy sleep pattern into your routine. Aim for at least seven hours of sleep every night. Listen to music that raises your spirits and helps you to maintain a calm demeanour. Avoid songs that remind you of anything unpleasant from your past or make you feel sad.

Eat healthy meals and drink plenty of water. Feeding your body a variety of nutritious foods, and in sensible quantities, will help you to regulate your weight, keep your mind sharp, and provide the energy to cope with the rigors of daily life. Regular consumption of good old H_2O will keep your brain and body hydrated which is essential for high performance. A bonus of good hydration is that it can help you to avoid unnecessary snacking.

Avoid watching and reading negative media sources. The press love nothing more than to stir up anything that creates a divide in our society or causes outrage through overinflated claims. Turning your back on all of this will have a big impact on your daily joy. If you go looking for news, search for stories that are: uplifting; that focus on our similarities; share joy; spread laughter; and send out a message of goodness.

Feed your brain with quality information from books and educational pursuits. You will gain valuable skills, feel satisfaction, and become more interesting to other people you hold conversations with. Never stop educating yourself. This world is crammed with amazing information and ideas that can inspire creativity and the willingness to learn within you.

Participate in a daily activity that raises your heartbeat. You do not need to purchase a gym membership or start marathon training, although if you do that is great, just go for a good walk and raise your heartbeat. Eventually, you will begin noticing the benefits to your health and you will start to enjoy and appreciate this exercise time.

When you want to enjoy the company of others, seek out good people. Those who are happy; who do not whine and moan; talk unkindly about others; love to laugh and enjoy themselves sensibly; and show you kindness.

Do something meaningful every day. This is your opportunity to do something for yourself. This could be anything such as: furthering your career; creating something beautiful; learning a new skill; getting some exercise. The possibilities are endless. Do what feels right for you and allow yourself to enjoy the moment.

Conduct

Be mindful of how you communicate with others. Using quality speech and body language will allow you to get across exactly what you want to say, how you feel, and what you expect from the group or person with whom you are conversing. It will also do wonders for your confidence and open doors of opportunity for personal and professional relationships.

How you react can have an impact on your life. Even if you are the nicest person anyone could meet when you are calm, if you explode into a fit of rage when things do not go your way then you should expect those who know you to be wary in your presence; and avoid your company. Refrain from losing your temper and instead look for anything that you can learn from the situation and/or improve upon. This will be a far better use of your time and keep your relationships healthy. If you believe that you cannot control your temper because it is part of your personality, then firstly, why on earth would you want this trait to be part of your personality? Secondly, you absolutely can train and control your feelings and emotions, and thirdly, there is categorically no shame in seeking professional help to better yourself.

Work Ethic

Whatever task is in front of you, just keep trying and persevering until you are successful. If you maintain this attitude, over time you will create a habit of pursuing excellence which will take you to the next level. Ensure that you follow through with what you decide to devote your precious time to.

Just remember that when it comes to learning something, be it an instrument, a language etc. it will take time; in some cases, years of practice and/or study. Be kind to yourself and do not heap pressure upon your shoulders. Keep going. It will be worth the effort in so many different ways.

Feeling satisfaction, and the motivation to go further, is an excellent indicator that your work ethic is strong. We all instinctively know when we are letting ourselves down and it is not a pleasant feeling. So, do whatever it takes to put in the effort, so you always feel a sense of achievement.

MIRROR TALK

Dedicate a small portion of your time every day to talk to yourself, using your affirmations, directly in the mirror. I appreciate that the idea of performing such an act might sound strange, but it is a fantastic way for you to understand how you are feeling, to stop negative inner dialogue, and to give yourself some self-care.

We talk to ourselves regularly every day confirming facts, ideas, and other areas of life, like how we think about our confidence or abilities. For many people this inner voice is one of negativity and fear. When we constantly affirm something negative to ourselves then we experience unwanted feelings repeatedly, and that is quite clearly not good for our mental health.

You must work hard to remove this behaviour and that is where looking into the mirror and addressing yourself will help. I appreciate that you might feel a sense of awkwardness at the idea of talking to yourself in the mirror, but I assure you that it will do wonders for your confidence and allow you to see yourself in a more positive light.

It might sound obvious and a confusing to be told how to talk to yourself in front of a mirror, but there is more to it than simply staring at your reflection and muttering a few words of encouragement. It all depends on what you need to tell yourself. Imagine that you are lacking in confidence. Initially, you might notice that your shoulders are drooping, and your eyes lack passion. Noticing your initial posture is an important step. Next, really focus on how you are feeling. Be honest and do not suppress the truth about how you feel. This will allow you to see firsthand how your thoughts are negatively affecting you. What would you say to yourself in this situation? A good place to start would be to tell yourself to stand up straight and pin your shoulders back, and to never treat yourself in such a manner ever again. Start saying things that boost your self-esteem. If you find that you feel annoyed at yourself, use the experience in a positive manner: *From this moment and beyond, I know that I am not good enough. I can achieve anything that I put my mind to.* Allow your words to be filled with passion. Explain to your reflection every quality that you possess, and any relevant past experiences that debunk the idea that you lack the confidence to succeed. Talk with your reflection for as long as required. Treat this exercise as if you were talking to someone you truly love and feel a deep sense of care towards; because that is exactly how you should feel about yourself.

There are many wonderful benefits to mirror talking. By talking face-to-face with your reflection, you will build a foundation for success, confidence, resilience and determination whilst also creating better communication skills regarding your feelings. It can help you to fight through times of great difficulty by allowing you to express your emotions and feelings, giving you an opportunity to move forward. It will help you to figure out what is important to you and exactly what you want to achieve in life. As a result, you will appear stronger and better in the eyes of others.

WHAT IS A POSITIVE AFFIRMATION?

Positive affirmations are words that you tell yourself to boost how you are feeling, attract positivity into your life, and help you to achieve your goals. These can be written down, read, listened to, or simply repeated in your head. Positive affirmations, when repeated consistently, can reshape your thoughts and even influence your behavior.

Affirmations are responsible for helping thousands of people make important changes in their lives. They work because they have the ability to reprogram your mind into accessing and believing the repeated statements and ideas.

There are many benefits of using positive affirmations, which include their ability to:

- Motivate you to take action and boost your desire to continue your actions.

- Influence your subconscious mind to access new beliefs and ideas.

- Change your negative thought patterns into positive ones.

- Help you feel positive about yourself and boost your self-confidence.

- Concentrate on your goals. Success is helped by persistently keeping your mind focused on what you want to succeed in.

HOW TO USE AFFIRMATIONS

When using affirmations, you must set aside a time during the day when you will not be disturbed. I find that first thing in the morning is a great time as it sets me up for a great day. Do not rush this time that you have chosen. You need to visualize and truly focus on the words that you speak.

When choosing affirmations from this book, feel free to play around with the words so they fully support your needs. This moment is all about your wellbeing and defining your goals, so never feel bad about setting this time aside. After all, how can you give love and kindness to others if you cannot give it to yourself?

This is an effective routine that you can use as you begin your affirmation journey:

- Stand in front of a mirror and look yourself in the eyes with kindness. Smile, if it feels natural to you. Stand up straight and push your shoulders back; have a confident and relaxed posture.
- Take three deep breaths, inhaling and exhaling to a count of three seconds breath in, three seconds hold, and three seconds breath out.
- Say your affirmations slowly and clearly. Repeat the affirmations three times, really focusing on the meaning of each word. Notice how your facial expression changes as you say the words. As an example, do you go from looking timid to appearing self-assured? Noticing and encouraging these changes is very important.
- Finally, notice how you feel inside. How has it affected you positively? Take another three

deep breaths, using the three second method at the start, allowing your body to absorb the positive feeling of the affirmation(s).

It is vitally important that any affirmation is worded properly. Using negative language such: *I can't, I won't*, are detrimental. Does the following sentence sound like a positive affirmation to you? *I'm going to stop having negative thoughts because they make me feel sad.* If we change the wording in this sentence, it becomes wholesome and inspiring: *I choose to focus my attention on happy thoughts because life is so amazing.*

As a small exercise, read those sentences again and notice the difference in how they make you feel.

AFFIRMATIONS

HAPPINESS AND JOY

I choose to be happy.

I deserve happiness and joy and I welcome it into my heart.

I am living in bliss.

Happiness comes to me easily.

Feeling joy comes naturally to me.

I am blessed with joy and happiness.

My heart is full of joy.

Smiling fills my life with happiness.

I bring joy to the people around me.

Every day brings me more joy and happiness.

I find happiness in every situation.

The happiness of others gives me so much joy.

My life overflows with joy.

I find joy in the simplest of pleasures.

I attract happy people to enjoy life with me.

I am a magnet for happiness, miracles and joy.

I already have everything I need to be happy within my soul.

The energy of happiness and bliss courses through every fibre of my being.

My heart is open and welcomes more happiness into my life.

I am creating a joyful life, full of wonder.

Every day I feel happier and happier.

I constantly notice how happy and positive I am.

I give myself permission to be happy.

CONFIDENCE AND SELF-BELIEF

I have full confidence in my ability.

I believe in myself at all times.

I am always in control of my life.

My self-belief is unshakable.

My confidence is constantly increasing.

My confidence inspires the others to be at their best.

Every day I wake up feeling confident and empowered.

I am so happy and grateful for my confidence.

I radiate self-confidence.

I have an abundance of great potential.

I am comfortable with expressing my confidence.

I accept and appreciate myself.

I am in full control of my life.

I realize that confidence is available to everyone, including me.

Confidence is always available to me.

My confidence is contagious.

I enjoy watching myself become more and more confident.

I have the confidence and self-belief in myself to change my life.

The only validation that I need is from myself.

I acknowledge my self-worth.

I see confidence and self-belief in my own eyes.

I can overcome anything.

My heart is full of belief in myself.

MOTIVATION AND SUCCESS

I am an unstoppable force of nature.

I am brimming with ambition.

My motivation to succeed is powerful.

I am worthy of success.

I expect excellence from myself.

My focus is razor sharp.

I thrive in high pressure situations.

I am a leader.

I set the standard of excellence.

I see challenge as an opportunity to become stronger.

I keep going until I hit my goals.

I have the power to get back up and keep going.

I reach my targets through hard work and dedication.

I am fully committed to my success.

I thoroughly enjoy a challenge.

I use my full potential.

I feel passionate about my work and always give my all.

I have the courage to stand out and shine.

Opportunity is always finding its way to me.

My attitude creates an abundance of opportunities for progression.

My positive behaviour is a source of great inspiration for others.

I feel calm, motivated, and powerful.

I have the power to create all the success that I desire.

Others look up to me because I am a leader.

I am trusted by others because I trust myself.

I surround myself with, and attract, positive people who help me to achieve my goals.

I honor myself by doing my very best.

SELF-LOVE

I love who I am.

I am so happy to be me.

I love my life more and more every day.

I am really enjoying the person I am becoming.

I am enough.

I deserve love.

I am love.

Love courses through every inch of my body.

I accept myself completely.

I am so grateful that I am alive.

My heart is full of love and compassion.

I accept praise and compliments with humility and gratitude.

I am surrounded by unconditional love.

I am my best friend.

I only say things about myself that are true, encourage, and support my highest good.

I show myself kindness and understanding.

I have a strong set of values and standards.

My mind, body, and soul are filled with love and respect for myself.

Love is a gift that I accept with gratitude.

I love myself unconditionally.

I have trust in myself; therefore, I am at peace.

I treat myself like a best friend should.

I love discovering new sides to my character.

I am so calm and peaceful.

LEARNING AND ACHIEVEMENT

I can achieve anything that I put my mind to.

I am going to achieve everything I have planned today.

I learn with an open mind.

I enjoy educating myself.

I receive tremendous pleasure from achievement.

Everything positive that I learn makes me a more interesting person.

Study is increasing my knowledge.

I easily absorb quality information.

I really enjoy learning new and interesting topics.

I am devoted to bettering myself.

Today I am going to learn something new and relish the experience.

I am becoming more intelligent every day.

I remember information easily.

I achieve my learning goals through my dedication and focus.

My desire to learn is immense.

I am open to better ways of learning.

Every achievement provides me with a new learning opportunity.

Today is a day that I fill with achievements.

I am persistent and fully focused on learning.

I take action to achieve my learning goals every day.

I can achieve this, and I will.

I am so grateful for everything that I have learned.

I am excited that I will learn something new today.

I am persistent and always find the answer.

I relish the challenges that learning brings.

I choose to put my studies first.

WEALTH AND ABUNDANCE

I attract wealth easily and in ever increasing quantities.

Money comes to me effortlessly.

Prosperity and abundance are attracted to me.

I am worthy of making more money.

My thoughts are of abundance.

Wealth, prosperity, and abundance constantly flow into my life.

My actions attract money.

Money finds its way to me expectantly and unexpectedly.

I am a money master and use it to create more wealth.

Wealth and abundance create further joy in my life.

My finances improve daily.

Money creates positive opportunities for me.

I am easily able to handle wealth.

Money pours into my life.

I am enjoying my journey in abundance.

I see abundance all around me.

I allow prosperity to flow into my life.

I learn more about growing my wealth daily.

Money allows me to live my life on my terms.

I have the capacity to grow my wealth grows every day.

I make positive decisions with my money.

Financial success belongs to me.

I am grateful for my wealth.

I make positive changes to the world with my money.

I am focused on my money goals.

I am abundance.

I am so thankful for all the wealth and abundance

coming my way.

HEALTH AND WELLNESS

I am looking after my physical and mental health
in the very best way.

My health and fitness are important to me.

I radiate good health.

I choose to eat healthy and wholesome foods.

I am in control of how I think, how I feel, and how
I live.

My mind is a temple of positive thought.

I make good choices about my overall health.

My mind has the ability to heal my inner self.

I live my best life for my health and wellbeing.

My mind is always calm.

I am healed.

I feel healthy and vibrant.

It is my choice how I feel right now.

My body and mind are healthy and at peace.

My heart and my mind are in sync.

I always make time for the things that make me feel good physically, mentally, and spiritually.

I am energetic, feeling great, and healthy.

I am so thankful for my health.

My immune system is strong.

Every day I am becoming fitter and healthier.

I pay attention to how I treat my body.

I feed my body wholesome and nourishing foods.

I enjoy making delicious and healthy meals.

I sleep peacefully and plentifully.

I let go of stress easily.

FORGIVENESS

I let go of the past and forgive myself.

I set my conscience free from any guilt and shame.

I never brood over my mistakes.

I learn from my mistakes and use such experiences to live a better life.

I am at peace with my past.

I show myself patience and understanding.

Forgiving myself makes it easier for me to forgive others.

I no longer accept beating myself up over what has happened in the past.

I am forgiven.

I swap my anger and shame for compassion, love and understanding.

I no longer feel shame.

I accept my mistakes and my decision is to move on.

I refuse to feel guilt anymore.

I refuse to feel shame anymore.

I allow my heart and mind to let go and heal.

I choose to love who I am and reject all feelings of hatred.

I take full responsibility for my choices and am grateful for the lessons I have learned.

I release all stress and tension from my life and embrace peace.

I let go of any feelings that do not serve my highest good.

I am worthy of the kindness and compassion found in forgiveness.

I am taking the necessary action to be a better version of myself.

I accept that I am not perfect.

Negative energy is not welcome in my life.

I release the pain of the past.

I no longer punish myself for past offences.

As I forgive myself it becomes easy to forgive others.

Right now, is where I start living a fresh, new life.

I open my heart to the power of forgiveness.

I am now mindful of my decisions and actions.

I move through forgiveness to embrace love.

I refuse to be a victim and claim my power.

I stop, right now, old behaviour patterns that do not serve my best life.

Forgiveness is a beautiful gift I give to myself with kindness and accept with love.

I am focused on a wonderful life in the present.

GRATITUDE

I am so happy and grateful for the wonderful gift of life.

I am grateful to be the good person that I am.

My heart and soul are full of gratitude for the love and friendship in my life.

The gratitude that I am showing allows me to see all the opportunities presented to me.

I am thankful that I enrich the lives of others.

I always appreciate and cherish the results of my hard work and effort.

My gratitude attracts miracles into my life.

Every morning I wake up feeling thankful.

I am so grateful for everything that I receive.

I am so thankful for the earth beneath my feet
and the air in my lungs.

Things keep getting better and better for me, and
for that I am grateful.

I am so happy and grateful that my life keeps
heading in the right direction.

I am grateful for those I love and who love me
back.

I am so thankful for the roof over my head and the
food on my plate.

I am so grateful for yesterday, today, and tomorrow.

I am grateful that I can feel so many beautiful feelings and emotions.

I am so thankful for all the lessons that I have learned in life.

I am grateful to be alive.

I am so happy and grateful for simply being myself.

WHO DO YOU WANT TO BE?

This is your opportunity to write down anything about yourself that you want to change, improve, or add to your life that is in line with your highest good; using the blank pages provided in. Also use this section to write about your feelings so you can reflect on anything that is having an impact on your life, from a good or not so good perspective.

Use the information that you write down as a source of inspiration; motivation to push forward and succeed; and as a welcome reminder of what you want and do not want. It will also give you the opportunity to track your progress.

The key is total honesty. Look deep inside your heart and discover the courage and integrity to not hold back about who you want to be and what you must do in order for this change to happen. Through this honesty, your mind will open, your heart will fill with self-love, and your shoulders will no longer carry any burden.

I CHOOSE TO BE...

I CHOOSE TO BE...

I CHOOSE TO BE...

PERSONAL AFFIRMATIONS

In this section you are encouraged to create your own affirmations using the blank pages provided. If you want to use the ideas in this book, without writing your own, that is fine. However, I would encourage you to personalize your own set as they will be empowered with, and tailored to, your vision and energy.

Enjoy yourself whilst creating your very own affirmations. Remember to be aware of the language that you use when writing. **KEEP IT POSITIVE!**

MY AFFIRMATIONS

MY AFFIRMATIONS

MY AFFIRMATIONS

MY AFFIRMATIONS

FINAL THOUGHTS

Positive affirmations are incredibly powerful. They release you from negativity, fear, worry, and anxiety. When these affirmations are repeated, they take charge of your thoughts, slowly changing your pattern of thinking and ultimately changing your life.

The way that you think is a matter of **CHOICE**. Always remember this fact:

IF YOU ARE THINKING NEGATIVE THOUGHTS, YOU HAVE THE POWER TO CHANGE THEM.

Just remember that harboring pessimistic, defeatist, and gloomy ideas can have a major impact upon your health.

Keep in mind that Rome was not built in a day, therefore, you must practice patience, kindness, and understanding towards yourself; be

CONSISTENT. Never give up creating the life that you want to live.

For in-depth advice on creating positive change, check out my book: *Take Action and Change: Be the Best Version of Yourself.* Which provides essential reading on the key areas of life that are important to get right. It has received 5-star reviews and has helped other people to change their life for the better.

ENJOY YOUR LIFE, BE BLESSED, AND BE HAPPY!

Printed in Great Britain
by Amazon

51807268R00040